The Elves and the Shoemaker

retold by FREYA LITTLEDALE

pictures by BRINTON TURKLE

Scholastic Inc.
New York Toronto London Auckland Sydney

For Dorothy

ISBN 0-590-41463-1

Text copyright © 1975 by Freya Littledale.
Illustrations copyright © 1975 by Brinton Turkle.
All rights reserved. This edition published by
Scholastic Inc.

12 11 10 9 8 7 6 5 4 3   8 9/8 0 1/9

There was once a good shoemaker
who became very poor.

At last he had only one piece of leather
to make one pair of shoes.

"Well," said the shoemaker to his wife,
"I will cut the leather tonight
and make the shoes in the morning."

The next morning he went to his table,
and he couldn't believe what he saw.

The leather was polished.
The sewing was done.
And there was a fine pair of shoes!
Not one stitch was out of place.

"Do you see what I see?" asked the shoemaker.

"Indeed I do," said his wife.
"I see a fine pair of shoes."

"But who could have made them?" the shoemaker said.

"It's just like magic!" said his wife.

At that very moment a man came in
with a top hat and cane.
"Those shoes look right for me," said the man.

And so they were.
They were right from heel to toe.

"How much do they cost?"

"One gold coin," said the shoemaker.

"I'll give you two," said the man.

And he went on his way
with a smile on his face
and the new shoes on his feet.

"Well, well," said the shoemaker,
"now I can buy leather for two pairs of shoes."
And he cut the leather that night
so he could make the shoes in the morning.

The next morning the shoemaker woke up,
and he found two pairs of ladies' shoes.
They were shining in the sunlight.

"Who is making these shoes?" said the shoemaker.
"They are the best shoes in the world."

At that very moment two ladies came in.
They looked exactly alike.
"My, what pretty shoes!" said the ladies.
"They will surely fit us."

And the ladies were right.

They gave the shoemaker four gold coins
and away they went . . .
clickety-clack, clickety-clack
in their pretty new shoes.

And so it went.
Every night the shoemaker cut the leather.
Every morning the shoes were made.

And every day more people came
to buy his beautiful shoes.

Just before Christmas the shoemaker said,
"Whoever is making these shoes
is making us very happy."

"And rich," said his wife.

"Let us stay up
and see who it is," the shoemaker said.

"Good," said his wife.
So they hid behind some coats,
and they waited and waited and waited.

When the clock struck twelve,
in came two little elves.
"*Elves*," cried the shoemaker.

"Shh!" said his wife.

At once the elves hopped up on the table
and set to work.

Tap-tap went their hammers.
Snip-snap went their scissors.
Stitch-stitch went their needles.

Their tiny fingers moved so fast
the shoemaker and his wife could hardly
believe their eyes.

The elves sewed and they hammered
and they didn't stop until all the shoes were finished.
There were little shoes and big ones.
There were white ones and black ones and brown ones.

The elves lined them all in a row.
Then they jumped down from the table.
They ran across the room
and out the door.

The next morning the wife said,
"The elves have made us very happy.
I want to make them happy too.
They need new clothes to keep warm.

So I'll make them pants and shirts and coats.
And I'll knit them socks and hats.
You can make them each a pair of shoes."

"Yes, yes!" said the shoemaker.
And they went right to work.

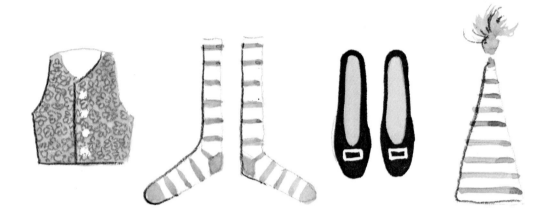

On Christmas Eve the shoemaker left no leather on the table.
He left all the pretty gifts instead.

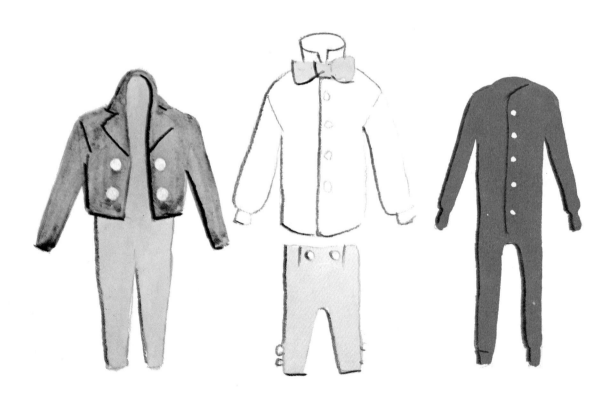

Then he and his wife hid behind the coats
to see what the elves would do.

When the clock struck twelve,
in came the elves, ready to set to work.

But when they looked at the table
and saw the fine clothes,
they laughed and clapped their hands.

"How happy they are!" said the shoemaker's wife.

"Shhh," said her husband.

The elves put on the clothes,
looked in the mirror,
and began to sing:

What fine and handsome elves are we,
No longer cobblers will we be.
From now on we'll dance and play,
Into the woods and far away.

They hopped over the table
and jumped over the chairs.

They skipped all around the room,
danced out the door,
and were never seen again.

But from that night on
everything always went well
for the good shoemaker and his wife.